HAND-MADE BOOKS

An introduction to bookbinding

To Ciara and Max

HAND-MADE BOOKS

An introduction to bookbinding

ROB SHEPHERD

SEARCH PRESS

First published in Great Britain 1994

Search Press Limited
Wellwood, North Farm Road,
Tunbridge Wells, Kent TN2 3DR

Text copyright © Rob Shepherd 1994

Photograph by Search Press Studios
Photographs and diagrams copyright © Search Press 1994

The author would like to thank the staff of Shepherds
Bookbinders for their support and permission to use the
Carte Decorate range of papers; Anne Muir Marbling for
the use of her papers; Katherine Brett of Payhembury
Papers; the fabric designers Bently and Spens for their
cloths.

ISBN 0 85532 754 5

If you have difficulty in obtaining any of the materials
or equipment mentioned in this book, please write for
further information to the publishers.
Search Press Limited, Wellwood, North Farm Road,
Tunbridge Wells, Kent TN2 3DR, England

Colour Separation By P&W Graphics, Singapore.
Printed in Spain by Elkar S. Coop, 48012, Bilbao.

Contents

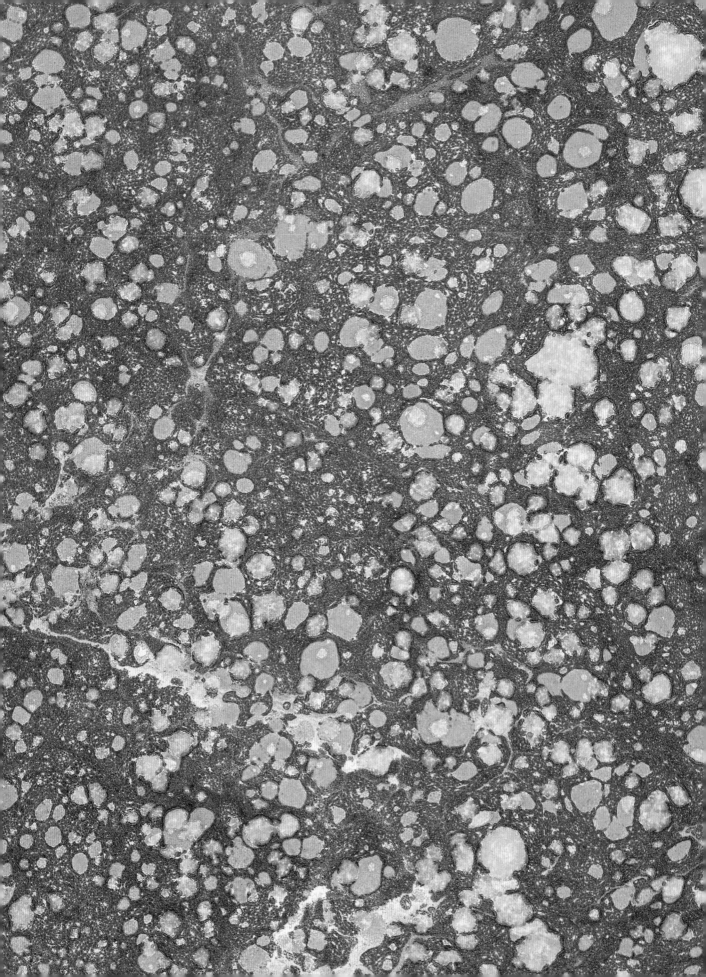

INTRODUCTION

*Books are not like other possessions;
they have a significance that sets
them apart from everyday objects.
Think for a moment about your own
bookshelves: there may be a collection
of well-thumbed paperbacks; some old
editions of books that are no longer in
print; a few old diaries; a photograph
album or two; and even some old
address books.*

Three traditional styles (front to back): a small quarter-bound notebook, a half-bound journal and a full-bound scrapbook.

Introduction

Despite all the technological advances in communication, books still play an important role in our lives. Perhaps this could be one reason why bookbinding is such an immensely satisfying and unique craft. Mass-production has certainly changed the way most books are bound, but there are still a few bookbinders who continue to use traditional methods to make books by hand.

The aim of this book is to introduce the beginner to the basic techniques and principles of bookbinding. Taking up any craft for the first time can be an unnerving experience. Bookbinding tools and particularly some of the more specialised materials can be expensive and difficult to obtain and, for someone working at home, bulky equipment can make considerable demands on space. For the beginner, however, special equipment is not necessary, and everything in this book can be made at the kitchen table.

The ten projects that I have included are designed to show the large range of books that can be made with the minimum of equipment. They concentrate on the use of paper and fabrics – materials that are readily available and come in an infinite variety of forms. Some of the very best bindings can also be the simplest; the combination of a well-made structure and carefully chosen materials can produce bindings of great style.

Other aspects of the craft, such as the use of leather and gold-tooling, should be left for a much later stage. However, simple and effective methods of titling can be used with all these projects (see page 22).

Bookbinding is a very old craft and over the centuries many binding styles have evolved. There are no absolute methods. No two bookbinders ever go about a task in the same way, nor indeed should they. Techniques are only a means to an end and, in the final analysis, it is the creative process that can bring much enjoyment and satisfaction. But remember, this book is only the beginning . . .

Design

The techniques for making books described in this book have been deliberately chosen for their simplicity and versatility. Each project demonstrates a basic technique and, as the illustrations of completed books show, it is the choice of materials and the proportions in which they are used that are the critical factors.

When making a book, it is important to choose materials that will be suitable in both weight and flexibility for the size and type of binding. For example, heavy furnishing fabrics are normally better suited to making portfolios than binding notebooks. On the other hand, a thin silk could be too light for some books unless it is lined with a paper backing sheet.

There should, however, be no absolute rules when it comes to the design or the choice of suitable materials for a binding. The combination of the unusual and the daring can make wonderful books.

Traditional styles

This book concentrates on three basic styles of bindings. The terms full, half and quarter bindings have their origins far back in bookbinding history.

Several hundred years ago books were full-bound in leather or vellum. These were, and still are, expensive materials and as time passed styles were adopted which used them only on the spine and corners (the points of maximum wear); these became known as half bindings. A further adaptation introduced the quarter binding, where the leather was used only on the spines. For the latter two styles the sides of the book were covered in marbled or printed paper and later on in cloth.

For the modern binder, half and quarter bindings provide a good format for experimenting with design ideas. They work best when the covering materials are in strong contrast to one another. By using different materials an infinite variety of textures, colours and patterns can be combined to produce unique and attractive bindings.

It is worth experimenting by making simple sketches, varying the proportions of the spine and corners relative to the overall size of the cover. Try and visualise the relationship of various combinations of fabrics and papers before deciding what style to adopt for a particular project.

If using a cloth or paper with a large pattern, it can be very helpful to cut some tracing paper to the required shape and size of the board area to be covered. Move this over the pattern to determine the best cut, but do remember to allow a little extra for the turn-ins.

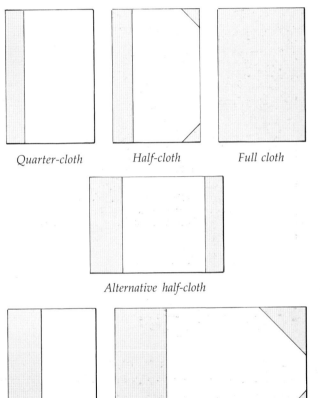

Quarter-cloth   *Half-cloth*   *Full cloth*

Alternative half-cloth

Experiment with different formats

If using a cloth or paper with a large pattern cut some tracing paper to the required shape and move this over the pattern to determine the best cut; allow a little extra for the turn-ins.

TOOLS AND MATERIALS

The following pages illustrate the tools and materials used to make the projects in this book. Many of the papers and fabrics are produced originally for quite different purposes but can be adapted quite effectively for bookbinding projects.

General handtools

Some of these handtools, such as the hammer and shears, are made specifically for the trade but can be substituted with similar items found in the home.

Saw – a small tenon saw for making cuts in some single-leaf types of bookblocks.

Ruler – a steel or steel-edged ruler is recommended when trimming materials with scalpels or craft knives. You can obtain non-slip straight-edges designed specifically for this purpose.

Cutting mat – a self-healing mat is a very useful tool when cutting paper and board. Alternatively, a piece of thick card can be used to protect the work surface.

Scissors – the pair illustrated are bookbinder's shears, but any good-sized, sharp scissors will be sufficient.

Knives – a scalpel and/or craft knife for trimming materials to shape; a small penknife with a slightly dull blade; a sharp flat-bladed knife for slicing folded sheets of paper.

Dividers – not essential, but very useful for scribing parallel lines prior to 'filling-in'.

Set square – to ensure that head and tail trims are square to the spine and fore-edge.

Needle – a strong, relatively large-eyed needle with a sharp point.

Pasting brushes – brushes with round heads are desirable for use with paste and PVA glue, but to get started flat decorators' brushes can be used.

Hammer – bookbinding hammers, as illustrated here, have a large round head but a normal woodworking hammer will suffice for the projects in this book.

Bodkin or awl – for making holes prior to sewing bookblocks.

Chisel – used to make slits for ribbons in portfolios.

Sponge and cloth – to dampen materials and keep work area clean.

Pencil and eraser.

Paper clips – for holding sheets together prior to sewing.

Folders/creasers – the best are bone, but you could use an old wooden ruler or the smooth handle of a spoon.

Other equipment

A variety of heavy weights and wooden pressing boards are particularly important for bookbinding projects. A small vice will also prove useful.

Vice – a small vice can be useful when working on the spine of small books.

Weights – a selection of weights, the heavier the better, for pressing paper and drying finished books.

Pressing boards – rectangular flat boards in a variety of sizes; off-cuts from timber merchants can be sanded smooth for this purpose.

Adhesives

The two glues recommended for use are PVA (polyvinyl acetate) and paste. They are normally used separately but for some projects they are mixed together. Both are available from bookbinding suppliers and PVA can be found in some hardware shops. Paste can be made at home from wheat flour (see recipe below).

PVA

In the bookbinding trade PVA has largely taken over from the traditional animal or 'Scotch' glues which are made from animal bones and require heating in a glue pot before they can be used. From the amateur's viewpoint, PVA has the dual advantages of being ready to use and, compared with the others, it is virtually odourless.

Another advantage of PVA is its flexibility when dry. This is important when gluing spines, where the adhesive requires a high degree of elasticity.

The disadvantage of PVA is that, unlike paste and animal glue, it is irreversible with moisture. This has little significance for the projects in this book but it is worth noting that, in general, PVA should not be used in restoration work where 'reversibility' is a first principle. However, some bookbinding suppliers do sell a special grade of reversible PVA.

PVA can be too thick and sticky for many applications and although it can be diluted with water, it works better when thinned with paste. The proportions of PVA to paste can be varied according to use.

Paste

Paste is the simplest and, in many ways, the finest bookbinding adhesive. It takes longer to dry than PVA, but makes a very strong bond. The following recipe is easy to make and, if kept in a cool place, will keep for several days. (Commercial paste contains preservatives which allow the paste to be kept for much longer.)

Wheat-flour paste

Wheat flour (not self-raising) makes a good paste, but corn (maize) or rice flour can also be used. The recipe uses six parts water to one part flour.

First, in an enamel or aluminium saucepan, mix the flour with a little of the water into a creamy consistency. Use a wooden spoon, and ensure all the lumps have disappeared before adding the remainder of the water. It saves time to heat the water in a kettle beforehand.

Stirring continuously, gently heat the mixture; the paste will gradually thicken as it comes to the boil. Turn down the heat and stir for a further minute while the mixture simmers, then remove from the heat and allow to cool.

To prevent a skin forming on the surface, cover with a piece of paper and a thin layer of water.

When the paste is cool, it is ready for use and should last for several days.

Mixing a general-purpose adhesive

For most of the projects in this book I recommend the use of the general-purpose mixture of PVA and paste.

Begin by dipping a brush into a bucket of PVA; then, using the lid of the glue pot (or a similar non-absorbent surface), work the PVA well into the body of the brush. Add a small amount of paste and, using a dabbing motion, mix the adhesives together on the lid. A downward dabbing action is the most effective method of mixing and applying glue. With this method the mixture can be freshened up or adjusted by adding either more paste or PVA.

Use a downwards dabbing action to mix PVA and paste.

Gluing paper and cloth

The handling of glue and the knowledge of how it affects materials are fundamental requirements for a successful binding. You will also need to appreciate the effects of the 'grain' of materials (see pages 19–20). Such understanding only comes with practice and it is important, therefore, to experiment with both PVA and paste and observe how different adhesives work when paper and cloth are glued to a board. Experiment with cheap papers before using more expensive ones.

When a sheet of paper, or any material for that matter, is covered with glue, the moisture in the adhesive causes the fibres to stretch. If the paper is then stuck to only one side of a piece of board, as the paper dries the fibres will contract and the board will bend. This bending, or 'warping', can only be counteracted by gluing a second piece of paper to the other side of the board.

Different papers, and materials such as cloth, will all vary in their degree of stretch, and this can be controlled to some extent by the choice of adhesive. PVA has a lower moisture content than paste and will therefore cause less warping.

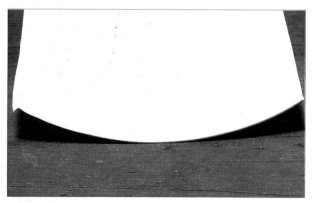

When a sheet of paper is stuck to one side of a board it will bow.

It is also very important to ensure that adhesive does not come into contact with the 'right' side of the paper or fabric. When gluing materials always use fresh sheets of waste paper underneath. Caution should be taken when using new newspapers as waste because sometimes the ink will offset and cause dirty marks.

Lining fabrics

To prevent glue from penetrating through to the face side of a fabric line it with a sheet of thin paper.

Stage 1

Cut a sheet of paper slightly larger than the piece of fabric on all sides. Using a general-purpose glue, glue-out the paper. Leave it for a few minutes until tacky. Before the adhesive is dry place the piece of fabric, face up, on to the glued surface and rub it down with a bone folder; the glue should not penetrate through to the face side of the cloth. A moist sponge will help remove remaining creases.

Stage 1.

Stage 2

Turn the laminate over and place it on a flat surface. Continue to rub with the bone folder to stretch the paper and remove all creases. The adhesive on the extremities of the paper should be allowed to stick to the board. As the paper dries it will shrink slightly and provide a relatively stiff bookcloth. When it is perfectly dry trim round the selvedge – the cloth can then be treated like a normal bookcloth.

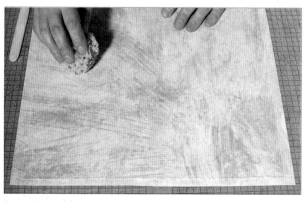

Stage 2.

Cloths

Bookcloths were first introduced into bookbinding in the 1820s as an alternative to leather. They are specially prepared to prevent adhesive from penetrating through to the face side but, if lined with paper as described, furnishing and clothing fabrics can be used very successfully.

Commercial bookcloths and buckrams – bookcloths can be bought by length from a roll, and are made in a variety of colours, weights and finishes. Almost all cloths are cotton-based and some, like washable buckrams, are water-resistant and particularly easy to use. However, bookcloths can be limited in their availability (only from book-binding suppliers) and in their range of designs and textures.

Mulls and calicoes – mull is a form of open-weaved muslin or scrim, and is used to line the spine sections of books. Calico, which is a form of light woven cloth, can be used for the same purpose. It is also useful for lining paper – decorative wrapping papers lined with calico are strong enough to be used as bookcloths. Both materials are available from bookbinding suppliers, fabric shops and haberdashers.

Furnishing and dress fabrics – almost any fabric can be used as a bookcloth, provided that the underside is first lined with a thin paper to prevent the penetration of glue during the binding process (see page 16).

Paper and boards

Paper and boards come in a variety of sizes, weights and colours, and the illustrations on these pages indicate some of the vast range of materials that are available. Like furnishing fabrics, many of these materials are produced originally for a completely different purposes but they can be used to good effect on bookbinding projects.

Paper can be purchased in a number of sheet sizes and consideration must always be given to the grain direction of a sheet and how it will run when the paper is folded (see below and page 26).

Paper weight is commonly measured in gsm units (grams per square metre) or in pounds (lb). The typical weight of a writing paper is around 90gsm (60lb), and a good weight for a large scrapbook would be 260gsm (120lb).

The best-quality paper is hand-made, particularly if made from cotton rag. It has strength and durability and a quality of surface that machine papers can never quite imitate.

Before the invention of paper-making machinery in the early part of the nineteenth century, all paper was made by hand. Its durability is clearly seen in books from the sixteenth and seventeenth centuries. The bindings may be coming apart but the paper often survives in almost perfect condition.

At the other end of the scale, the introduction of wood-pulp into the paper-making industry marked a sharp decline in standards. Much of the book production this century has been characterised by poor-quality paper. The acidity in the fibres causes the paper to weaken and, just like old newspapers, it turns yellow and brittle in a very short time.

Public awareness, and a change of direction within the industry, have reversed the downhill trend. There is certainly no shortage of interesting and diverse papers on the market, and these are often advertised as being 'acid-free'.

In choosing papers for bookbinding, quality is an important consideration but should not become a fixation. Interesting and useful books, such as lined-paper notebooks, can be made from the cheapest materials. Inexpensive wrapping papers often make excellent endpapers and covering papers.

Decorative papers – coloured or patterned sheets used for endpapers and covering. They include hand-made textured papers, traditional hand-marbled papers, printed wrapping paper and wallpaper.

Grain direction

Most materials have a 'grain direction' and it is important to spend a little time understanding this principle and its effects.

Utility papers – kraft paper (brown wrapping paper) and sugar paper are essential for most projects. Silicone-release paper (or greaseproof paper) and blotting paper are also very useful, as is a supply of old magazines and newspapers for gluing-out on.

Book papers – plain, lined, tinted and textured paper; available in many colours, weights and qualities.

Boards are available in a range of thicknesses.

Boards - millboard, greyboard, hardboard and plywood can all be used for the projects in this book. Millboard, the best-quality bookbinding board, is very dense and can be difficult to cut by hand. Greyboard is a lighter material which will cut easily; its strength can be enhanced by lining each side with paper. Hardboard and plywood are only used for making large portfolios.

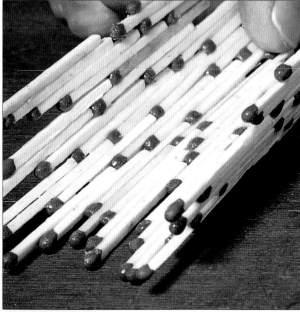

Matchsticks glued together to indicate grain fibres.

Moisten the edge of paper to check grain direction.

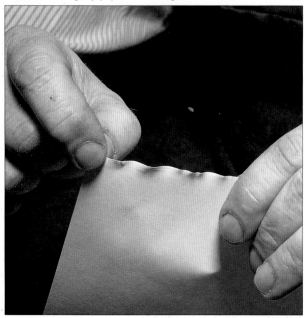

Drag finger and thumb along paper to check grain direction.

The general rule is that all materials should have their grain running from head to tail in the finished book. Failure to observe this rule can cause the book covers to warp when materials with opposing grains are glued together. Books with sewn sections always lie flatter, and open better, if the grain of the paper in the bookblock is running correctly.

Looked at under a microscope, the fibres of a material such as paper would be seen to lie in parallel lines, rather like logs floating down a river. These lines, or direction of flow, indicate the grain direction.

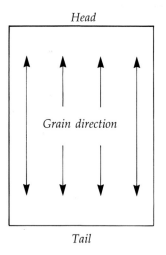

Head

Grain direction

Tail

To take the analogy a stage further, imagine a box of matchsticks spread out on a table and all pointing the same way. Now imagine them glued together. If you were to try and bend the matchsticks lengthways, against the grain, they would resist and yet if the matchsticks are bent in the other direction, across the direction of flow, they bend easily, as illustrated in the photograph.

The fibres which make up a piece of paper or board behave in exactly the same way. The direction in which there is greater resistance to bending is the grain direction. This method is more evident with boards, but there are a number of ways of testing papers for grain direction.

One is to moisten the edges of a sheet of paper at one corner. As the fibres absorb the moisture they expand. The edge running parallel with the fibres stretches with the grain and remains comparatively flat. Across the grain, however, the fibres have no space in which to stretch and this causes the paper to cockle.

Another way is to drag your finger and thumb along the edge of a piece of paper; again the amount of cockling will show the grain direction.

Sewing materials

Sewing materials also vary in type and below are illustrated some of the different types of threads, cords and ribbons you can use when binding books.

Where specialist materials, such as bookbinder's sewing thread, may be difficult to obtain, more readily available substitutes are given.

Thread – *as a general rule, sewing thread must be strong enough to support the paper but not so thick as to cause excessive swelling in the spine. The strongest thread is made from ready-waxed linen in a variety of thicknesses available from bookbinding suppliers. For light work, a 25/3 gauge will suffice, but for sewing magazines a thick gauge such as 18/3 would be more suitable.*

Ordinary linen thread can be bought from sewing shops and then waxed with bees-wax. For large books, waxed polyester or 'whipping twine' can be obtained from ships' chandlers. It comes in several gauges and is very strong.

Hemp – *available from bookbinding suppliers, ships' chandlers and hardware shops. Thin hemp is used in the chapter on repairing and making single-leaf bookblocks. Alternatively, any good-quality twine or string can be used.*

For small single-section bindings, coloured silk or polyester makes an attractive alternative.

Waxed dental floss also makes an excellent sewing material.

Bookbinding tapes – *available in sizes from 5–20mm (³/₁₆–³/₄in) in width. Linen ones are best, and for the projects in this book they are easier to use when they are a little stiff. Alternatively, strong cotton tapes can be bought from haberdashers and sewing shops.*

Silk threads and narrow ribbons make excellent bindings for the limp Japanese-type bindings.

Finishing materials

The term 'finishing' refers to the process of decorating and titling the covers of a book and is generally associated with the craft of gold-tooling on to leather covers. Finishing is often considered the most difficult part of bookbinding, but for books made from paper and cloth simple and effective titles can be made in the following ways.

A typed label is one simple method of adding a title to a book. Modern typewriters often have a choice of typefaces and by using a coloured paper a label can easily harmonise with the overall design of the book. The appearance and feel of a label can be enhanced by recessing a small panel on to the front cover board in which the label can sit.

Word processors, computers and typewriters can also be used to create titles and designs directly on to the covering materials. Obviously this must be done prior to making the case and some planning is needed to ensure the correct positioning of the design.

Calligraphy is another very effective way of titling and can be applied straight on to the cover paper or on to a label.

Rub-down lettering, available from most art and craft shops, comes in a wide variety of typefaces and decorative motifs but should only be used on a fairly smooth surface. To prevent the letters being rubbed off a protective varnish (PVA thinned with water) can be applied.

Book covers can be titled and decorated in all kinds of ways. Try experimenting with combinations of the above methods. Do not be afraid to take risks with your designs as a bold approach can often lead to the most exciting results.

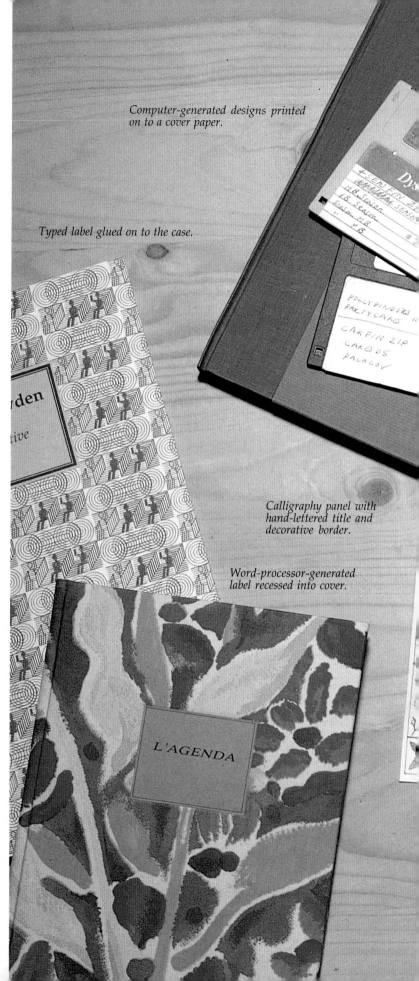

Computer-generated designs printed on to a cover paper.

Typed label glued on to the case.

Calligraphy panel with hand-lettered title and decorative border.

Word-processor-generated label recessed into cover.

Rub-down lettering is available
in many type styles, sizes
and colours.

George Orwell
Nineteen Eighty-Four

Penguin Modern Classics

1984

Recessed pieces of an
old paperback wrapper.
Photographs can also be
used in the same way.

Flowers

手帳

Hand-written label glued
on to cover.

SINGLE-SECTION BINDINGS

This chapter demonstrates the basic principles of single-section bookbinding, and although the techniques are relatively simple, it is possible to create useful and very attractive bindings. The first project is a small notebook finished in a 'quarter-cloth' style. The next is a slightly larger booklet with a half binding. Finally a full binding is applied to a sketchbook in which the bookblock is made from watercolour paper.

A quarter-cloth notebook

This book, in common with the other two projects in this chapter, comprises a single set of folded papers sewn together to form a 'bookblock'. The 'case' is constructed as a separate exercise and then the two are brought together and 'cased-in'.

The materials listed can be obtained from various sources, and thought should be given to the combination of colours and patterns and how they work together. When selecting materials care must be given to ensure that the grain of each material runs from head to tail in the finished book. It is the choice of materials that will give the binding style.

Making the bookblock

Stage 1

Take one sheet of paper at a time and carefully fold it in half as shown below. The edges of the paper should meet as closely as possible.

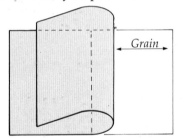

With a penknife slit each fold just beyond the halfway mark; slitting the paper in this way helps to prevent the paper creasing at the next fold.

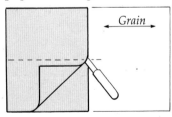

Now fold the sheets in half a second time, at 90° to the first, to form a four-leaf section.

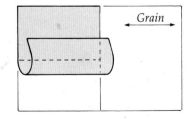

Materials

Five sheets of A4-size (about 12 x 8in) plain white typing or photocopying paper, with the grain running with the long edge, for the bookblock.

One sheet of plain coloured paper, the same size or slightly larger than the white, for the endpapers.

150 x 75mm (6 x 3in) piece of mull or calico (or any thin woven material).

500mm (18in) length of linen or strong polyester thread (or a coloured embroidery thread).

One sheet of patterned paper for the cover.

200 x 75mm (8 x 3in) piece of spine cloth.

One sheet of millboard or greyboard, 1–1.5mm (about 1/16in) thick, sized to allow the cutting of two cover boards slightly larger than the bookblock, with the grain running head to tail.

Fresh paste and PVA.

Take the coloured endpaper and fold it in a similar manner. The endpapers must be big enough to cover the bookblock and preferably slightly larger. They will be trimmed after sewing.

When all six sheets have been folded, open each four-leaf section at the middle and insert one into another, with the endpaper section on the outside. The result is a single twenty-four-leaf bookblock with the grain running from head to tail.

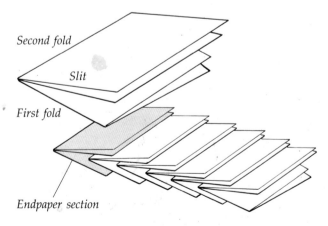

Second fold

Slit

First fold

Endpaper section

Stage 2.

Stage 2

Take the piece of mull or calico and fold it around the bookblock. Keeping the edges of the paper as level as possible, open the bookblock at the middle and insert paper clips at the head and tail of the pages to keep the materials in place – the book is now ready for sewing.

Stage 3

Hold the book half open and, using a sharp needle (or bodkin), make one hole at the centre of the fold and two others approximately 50mm (2in) on either side. If the bookblock is held over the edge of a wooden block or table, it will make it easier to guide the needle through the centre of the fold. The diagram below illustrates the route taken by the sewing thread in stages 5–7.

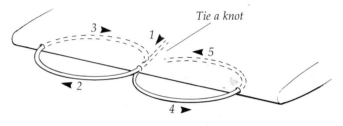

Stages 4a and 4b

Thread the needle. Push the linen thread through the eye of the needle, slightly unravel the thread, pass the point of the needle through and draw the 'knot' tight.

Stage 3.

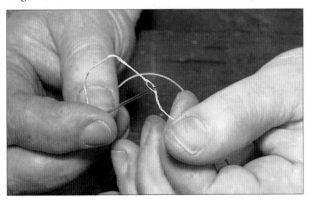
Stage 4a.

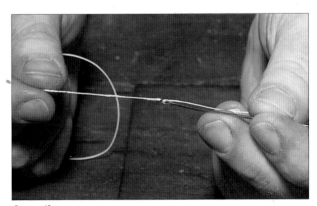
Stage 4b.

Stage 5.

Stage 6.

Stage 7.

Stage 5

Working from the inside of the bookblock, push the needle through the centre hole, back through one of the other holes and then out through the centre hole again.

Stage 6

Tighten any loops by pulling the thread parallel to the spine of the bookblock.

Stage 7

Now pass the needle through the third hole and join the thread to the loose end on the inside of the bookblock with a simple knot as shown in the diagram below. The ends should be trimmed off with 10mm (³/₈in) to spare.

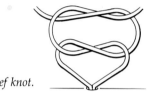

A simple reef knot.

Stage 8

With the sewing completed, the endpapers and bookblock can be trimmed. Start with the long edge or fore-edge. Flip through the pages to determine the unevenness of the edges. If the paper was folded neatly, only a small amount of trimming will be necessary. Determine the trimming point by eye and using dividers or a ruler, draw a pencil line on the endpaper parallel with the spine.

Trimming must be carried out with a sharp knife and steel-edged safety rule. It is only ever possible to cut thin books in this way and, even then, it may take several cuts with a knife to penetrate the layers of paper.

Stage 9

Align one side of a set square against the trimmed fore-edge and draw trimming lines at the head and tail of the bookblock.

Stage 10

Trim off the waste as described above. The bookblock is now complete and can be put to one side while you make its case.

Stage 8.

Stage 9.

Stage 10.

Making the case

Stage 1

Cut the cover boards and paper to sizes suitable for the bookblock as shown in the diagram.

The cover boards must allow a 5mm (³/₁₆in) overhang at head, tail and fore-edge for the 'squares', and an inset of 8mm (⁵/₁₆in) at the spine for the hinge. Check the grain direction. Boards can be cut by first measuring with a ruler or, alternatively, the cutting marks can be calculated by holding the bookblock against the board and marking off by eye. Use a set-square to achieve good right-angles.

The paper for the boards must have a 15mm (⁵/₈in) turn-in on all three sides. If using patterned paper, consider where the pattern will be positioned.

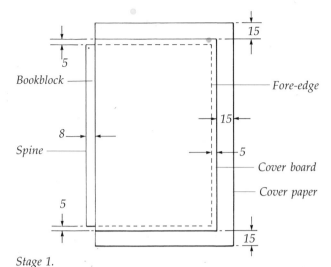

Stage 1.

Stage 2

Holding the bookblock and boards in position, take a piece of waste paper and wrap it around the spine. Using a pencil, mark off where the paper touches the edge of the boards. This will give a measurement for the spine width. Cut a piece of waste board to this width; this will serve as a gauge for positioning the cover boards. A gauge is particularly useful if you are making a number of books to the same size.

Make a pencil mark on each cover board at the point to which the cloth spine will overlap. Assemble the two boards with the spine gauge between and measure the distance between the pencil marks. Cut the width of spine cloth to this measurement. The length of the cloth should allow a 15mm (⁵/₈in) turn-in at the head and tail.

Stage 2.

Stage 3

Using PVA mixed with some paste, glue-out the cloth and position the spine gauge in the centre. Lay the boards against the gauge, taking care to keep them level at the head and tail. At this stage, the glue should have enough 'slip' to make any necessary adjustments. Remove the gauge.

Stage 3.

Stage 4

Without disturbing the covers, carefully turn in the spine cloth overlaps at head and tail and rub down with a bone folder. Take a little time to achieve good tight creases. Turn the assembly over so that the spine cloth is uppermost, rub down the spine cloth to remove any creases and then put to one side.

Stage 4.

Stage 5.

Stage 6.

Stage 7.

Stage 8.

Stage 5

Glue-out the cover paper, one sheet at a time, using a fresh sheet of waste paper beneath each.

Stage 6

'Pitch' each glued cover paper on to the cover boards. Paper when glued has a habit of curling and this can make positioning difficult. With the paper lying glued-side uppermost (to counteract any curl) turn the edge furthest from the spine over to meet the cloth edge. The paper should overlap the cloth by about 2mm ($^1/_{16}$in). When positioning the cover paper, take care to ensure that the edge runs parallel with the spine.

Stage 7

Before turning in the sides, cut the paper diagonally at about 2mm ($^1/_{16}$in) from the corners.

Stage 8

Turn in the head and tail and pinch the corners in with the fingernails or bone folder, before turning in the fore-edge. When turning cloth or paper over the boards, carefully stretch the material tightly over the edges. If necessary, apply more glue to the edges of the cover paper before turning in.

Turn the cover over and gently bone down the cover paper to eliminate any air pockets.

Let the case dry under a weight before casing in the bookblock. As the covering materials dry, the boards will want to bow (as described on page 16), so drying the case underneath a weight will help to keep it flat. Any bowing, however, will be counteracted when the book is cased-in.

Casing-in

The process of casing-in attaches the case to the bookblock and completes the binding.

Stage 1

Lay the dried-out case flat on the table with the outside facing down. Position the bookblock on one of the cover boards, ensuring that the squares are correct. Insert a piece of scrap newspaper under the first endpaper and glue the endpaper underneath the mull. Then, working outwards to the edges, glue-out the whole endpaper. Great care must be taken not to get glue on the edges of the paper of the bookblock.

Stage 2.

Stage 3.

Stage 4.

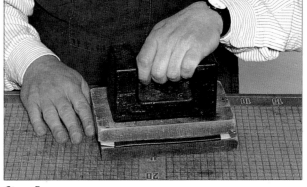

Stage 5.

Stage 2

Hold the bookblock in position and pull the cover board over to meet the glued paper.

Stage 3

Apply a little pressure with the palm of your hand, and then flip the book over. Keeping the glued board and endpaper flat against the surface, carefully lift the bookblock far enough to slip your hand in and adjust the position of the endpaper. The endpaper should lie reasonably square to the boards and, once you are satisfied with its position, rub the paper down with the tips of your fingers. Take care to rub the paper down well into the spine, but do not be tempted to lift the board too far back as this may cause the paper to cockle and crease.

Turn the book over and repeat the operation for the other endpaper.

Cut some silicone-release paper (or greaseproof), and insert between the inside boards and the free endpapers. This will stop any surplus glue from sticking where it should not, and also help to prevent moisture from the boards penetrating the bookblock.

Stage 4

With a bone folder, or similar tool, gently find the crease where the board edge becomes the spine and run the tool along to define the line for the hinge.

Stage 5

Put the book between pressing boards, and leave it to dry with a heavy weight on top for at least a day. A sheet of blotting paper inserted inside each board will help keep the book dry.

Half-cloth lined notebook

Most stationers and some newsagents carry cheap notebooks with lined paper. In this project a simple lined-paper booklet is used to make the bookblock of a more durable half-bound book. It is important to buy paper that has been folded at the centre. These will usually be stapled through the middle and incorporate a simple card cover on the outside. Ideally the grain of the lined paper should run from head to tail.

The method of construction is similar to that in the previous section but, for this book, a different type of endpaper is used and, of course, the case is a half binding.

Making the bookblock

Stage 1

Remove the staples from the folds of the lined-paper booklet, discard the covers and then knock up the edges of the paper up as square as possible. Ignoring the inclusion of endpapers, sew the bookblock through a single fold of mull as described on pages 27–28 and put to one side.

Fold each sheet of endpaper in half to form two two-leaf sections.

Materials

Lined-paper booklet, with about forty leaves, size approximately 200 x 165mm (8 x 6^1/$_2$in). Remove staples and discard limp cover.

Two sheets of plain coloured paper, slightly larger in size than an unfolded sheet of the lined paper, for the endpapers.

200 x 75mm (8 x 3in) piece of mull or calico (or any thin woven material).

500mm (18in) length of linen or strong polyester thread (or a coloured embroidery thread).

One sheet of patterned paper for the cover.

500 x 100mm (18 x 4in) piece of spine cloth, sufficient for the spine and corners.

One sheet of millboard or greyboard, 1–1.5mm (about ^{1}/$_{16}$in) thick, sized to allow the cutting of two cover boards slightly larger than the bookblock, with the grain running head to tail.

Fresh paste and PVA.

Take one folded sheet at a time and paste a thin line of glue, 5mm (^{1}/$_4$in) wide, along the folded edge. This is best achieved by holding a piece of waste paper along the line as a guard as shown.

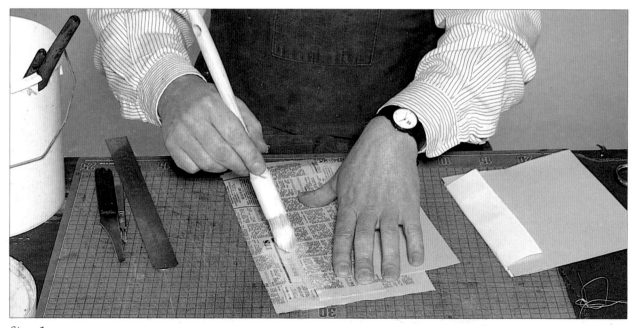

Stage 1.

Stage 2.

Stage 2

Tip in the endpaper, beneath the mull, on to the spine edge of the first and last pages of the bookblock.

Rub the glued edge to ensure a good join and then leave under a heavy weight for a few minutes. When the glue has dried check that the endpaper is stuck securely and, if necessary, pull it off and start again.

Stage 3

When they are dry and firmly attached the endpapers can be trimmed to the size of the block. Place your straight-edge between the lined paper and the bottom endpapers, align it with the fore-edge and trim off the excess paper. Repeat for head and tail and then turn the bookblock over and trim the other set of endpapers.

Stage 3.

Making the case

Making a case in a half-bound style requires a little more consideration about the design. The proportions will depend on your choice of materials. Draw lines on one of the boards to help you visualise the finished appearance.

Stage 1

When you have decided on the proportions a very simple corner template can be made from a piece of scrap board. Cut a straight edge on the scrap board and lay it underneath the pattern board aligned with the drawn diagonal. Cut the other sides of the template referring to the dimensions on the diagram below. Binders often keep templates of this sort and after a while they have a collection of most of the sizes required.

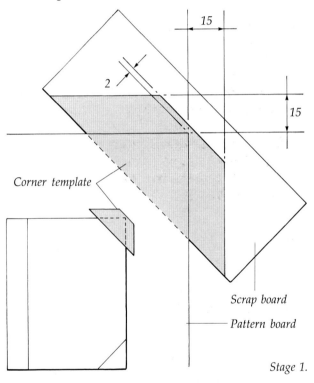

Corner template

Scrap board

Pattern board

Stage 1.

Cut the cover paper as for a quarter binding (see page 30) and position on the board with a small weight. Fold each corner back to determine the trim and crease with a bone folder. Using the crease as a guide, trim off the corners with a knife and straight-edge. The paper has to overlap the cloth at the spine and corners but the margin need only be small as the paper will stretch when glued. Before cutting a patterned cover paper, you should consider how the design will be positioned and, if necessary, use a tracing-paper template to locate the best cut.

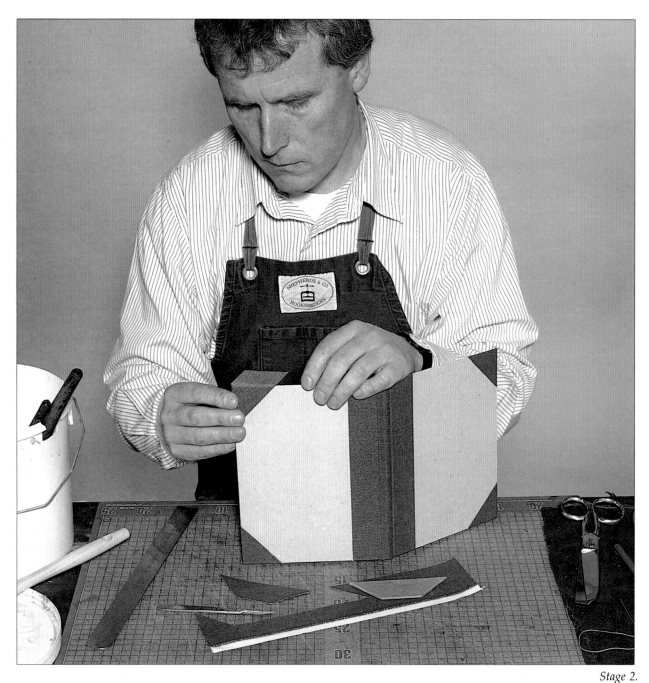

Stage 2.

Casing-in

Case-in the bookblock and cover as for the quarter-cloth notebook (see pages 32 and 33).

Stage 2

Make the case as described in stages 1–4 on page 30, and then fit the corners to the cover boards as shown above. Pinch in the corner folds as detailed in stage 8 on page 31.

Complete the case by pitching the cover paper on to the front and back cover boards.

Note An alternative covering method for a half-binding is described on page 40.

Full-bound traditional sketchbook

Single-section sewing, by definition, is only suitable for making books with a small number of pages. Although this is a limiting factor, it works particularly well when binding something requiring very specific and special paper, as in this exercise. Despite the relatively simple techniques, this style of binding can be made to a very fine specification. For the pages of this book a fine watercolour paper with a natural 'deckle-edge' has been chosen. The final size of the binding is determined by the size of the paper, as the deckle will not be trimmed.

The silk covering material is a clothing fabric and has first been lined, as described on page 16, to prevent glue from penetrating the material. Any clothing or furnishing fabric can be used, provided that the weave is not too open.

The endpapers are made from the first and last leaves of the bookblock; these are known in the trade as 'self-ends'. If you prefer, endpapers can be made from a different type of paper and bound in using either of the two methods previously described.

Materials

Three 760 x 560mm (30 x 22in) sheets of deckle-edge watercolour paper.

400 x 300mm (16 x 12in) piece of bookcloth or laminated fabric for the cover material.

1m (3ft) thread or silk embroidery thread.

250 x 100mm (10 x 4in) piece of mull.

One sheet of millboard or greyboard, 1–1.5mm (about 1/16in) thick, sized to allow the cutting of two cover boards slightly larger than the bookblock, with the grain running head to tail.

Fresh paste and PVA.

Endpapers (optional).

Two 250 x 200mm (10 x 8in) pieces of sugar paper or similar thickish paper for filling-in the inside of the covers. Grain must be head to tail.

Making the bookblock

The bookblock is made in a similar way to the book in the first project. The watercolour paper is folded and interleaved to form the required number of pages. After sewing, the folds can be slit with a blunt paper knife; a slightly ragged edge will complement the natural deckle edges.

As the size of the bookblock is quite large it is sewn through the mull using five holes rather than three. The diagram below illustrates this sewing pattern. As a decorative alternative to sewing thread, thin twine or silk embroidery thread can be used.

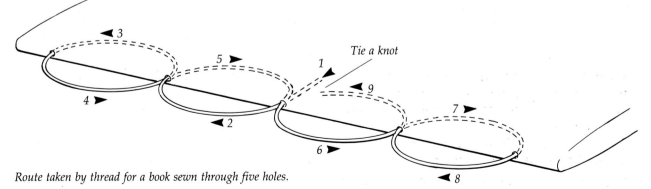

Route taken by thread for a book sewn through five holes.

Making the case

Making the case from a single piece of fabric is in one sense easier than either the half or quarter bindings. The only problem comes in gluing-out a single piece of cloth, especially if it is quite large; the fabric will tend to curl up as the adhesive soaks in and this can make handling difficult. This can be overcome to a great extent if you follow the procedure given below.

If you choose to use ordinary fabric, rather than book cloth, you will need to line it with a thin sheet of paper as described on page 16.

Stage 1

Lay the piece of cloth face down on the table. Lay the cover boards in position, making the appropriate allowance for the width of the spine, and draw around the edges of the boards with a pencil. Check that the top and bottom edges are parallel.

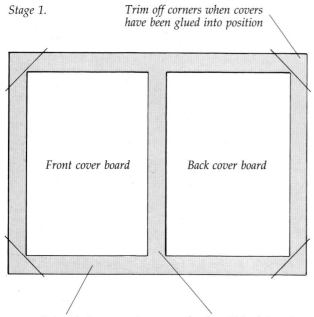

Stage 1.

Trim off corners when covers have been glued into position

Front cover board

Back cover board

Cover cloth

Leave gap for the width of the spine

Glue-out one half of the cloth and immediately lay one board in position. Glue-out the other half of the cloth and lay that board down. Turn the case over and gently rub down any creases or air pockets with a bone folder.

Turn the case over again. Using a sharp pair of scissors, trim out the corners, leaving a width of cloth a little greater than the thickness of the board (see stage 7 on page 31).

Stage 2.

Stage 2

Turn over the edges of the cover material, applying more glue if necessary. Start with the long edge (head or tail), and try to turn as much of the edge over as possible in one go. Stretch the cloth over to prevent air pockets on the edge of the boards. Rub down with a bone folder, especially at the spine, where you should rub well into the inside edges of the cover boards.

Filling-in

The appearance of the inside boards is just as important as that of the outside and in this project the unsightly edge of the turned-in cover cloth is eliminated by filling-in.

Stage 1

Lay the case open, with the inside uppermost, and trim out the turned-in cloth. A pair of dividers drawn down the edge of the cover board is a good way of marking parallel lines. Trim out the excess using a straight edge and knife.

Stage 1.

Stage 2

Cut a piece of sugar paper a little larger than the size of the space to be filled, with the grain direction running head to tail.

Using a sticky PVA, which will impart the minimum of stretch, glue-out one of the cover boards, taking care not to get any glue on the turned-in cover material.

It is important not to let the filling-in paper pull the boards too much, and for this reason it is better to glue the boards rather than the sugar paper.

Stage 2.

Casing-in – gluing the self-ends to the cover.

Stage 3

Butt the sugar paper flush against one of the turned-in edges of the cover material and lay down the complete sheet. Gently smooth down with your fingers.

Using a straight-edge and a sharp knife, trim the final edges *in situ* and rub well down. If you have chosen your paper thickness correctly the join should be quite flat to the touch. Although filling-in may not completely disguise the turn-ins, it is well worth the effort to reduce their effect and create even borders.

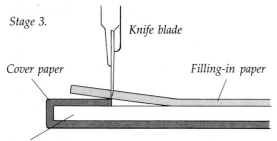

Stage 3.

Knife blade

Cover paper

Filling-in paper

Cover board

Casing-in

Casing-in is accomplished in a similar manner to that described on pages 32–33, but on this occasion the first and last leaves act as endpapers (self-ends).

Full binding with paper sides

Another method of creating a half-bound style is to cover the full-bound cloth case with a paper at the fore-edge or corners. This is a more wasteful method of making a half binding than that described earlier, but it has the advantage of not giving any unsightly ridges where the cloth and paper meet. However, consideration must be given to the 'pull' of two layers of material; filling-in will help to counteract any warping effect.

OPPOSITE: *Further examples of single-section bindings.*

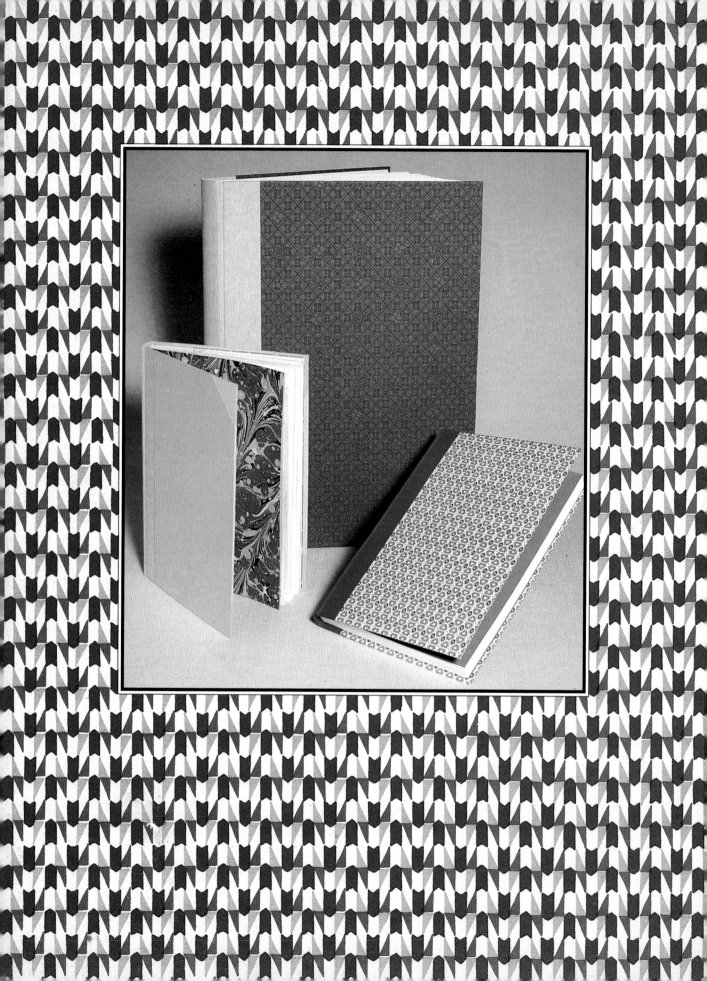

MULTI-SECTION BINDINGS

The size of most books will necessitate the use of two or more sections; these are known as multi-section bindings and three different types of sewing structures are explored in this chapter. The first is used for a multi-section lined-paper journal and the second for binding a set of magazines. The third structure involves the construction of a large scrapbook or photograph album.

Lined-paper journal

In this exercise a quarter-bound cover is used to case-in twelve sections of folded lined paper, purchased originally as simple booklets. It is also possible to use many other types of paper to achieve a similar result.

Making the bookblock

Stage 1

Separate the folded sheets of paper into the required number of leaves. For this project twelve twenty-four-leaf sections are used to make the bookblock.

Although the sections are pre-folded it is worth while spending a little time to reduce any swelling at the fold. This is achieved by gently tapping the folded spine of each section with a hammer.

Stage 1.

Stage 2

Swelling can also be reduced by placing all the sections between pressing boards and leaving them under a heavy weight for twenty-four hours. The sections should be stacked alternately, spine to fore-edge, to avoid all the folds being on the same side. This will also result in a flatter stack.

Stage 3

The next step is to 'knock up' the sections ready for sewing. Remove the sheets from under the weight and place the sections, with all the folds at one side, between two boards cut slightly larger than the paper size. These boards should be square at the ends and placed flush with the top edge of the book. Holding the stack firmly in both hands, tap the top edge down on to a flat surface. Loosen your grip slightly as the paper drops against the surface. This will allow the paper to fall level.

Stage 2.

Stage 3.

Stage 4.

Stage 4

Turn the block through 90° and repeat the action for the spine edge. Alternate this process between the top edge and the spine until the book feels level at both edges. Lay the bookblock flat on the table and, holding the book tight again, proceed to hammer along the edge of the boards to consolidate the folds. Knocking up sections in this way will result in a reasonably flat and level top to the book.

Lay the bookblock flat on its side with a heavy weight on top and make any final adjustments to the squareness using a set-square.

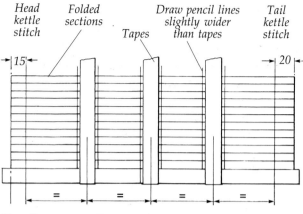

Head kettle stitch · Folded sections · Tapes · Draw pencil lines slightly wider than tapes · Tail kettle stitch

 15 · 20

Stage 5. *Tapes must be equi-spaced between kettle stitches*

Stage 6.

Stage 5

Mark the bookblock for sewing as shown in the diagram above. The first and last stitches, known as the kettle stitches, are placed about 15mm (⁵/₈in) from the top of the book, and about 20mm (³/₄in) from the tail. The three tapes are placed equidistant between the two kettle stitches. Mark the positions of the stitches and those of the sewing tapes in pencil on the spine fold of the top section. Draw vertical lines down over the other sections using the set-square. The pencil lines showing the position of the tapes are drawn a little wider than the actual width of the tapes.

Normally this type of sewing is accomplished with the aid of a sewing frame. However, it is quite easy to improvise by securing the tapes at the appropriate positions to a block of wood or the edge of a table.

Stage 6

Using some adhesive tape, secure the sewing tapes to the underside of a table, or a suitably sized block of wood, at the positions marked on the bookblock.

Remove the sections from under the weight and, working from the inside of each section, use a bodkin to punch a hole at each pencil mark (see stage 3 on page 27). This action is not absolutely necessary, but it will make your first few attempts at sewing books much easier.

When all the sections have been pierced at the correct points, knock up all the sections again as described in stages 3 and 4 and then lay the bookblock on the table or board, aligning the holes with the sewing tapes.

Stage 7

Thread the needle with one length of thread and knot the end as shown on page 27. Working on the last section of the bookblock, take the needle in through the tail kettle stitch and out through the second hole (see diagram below). Hold the section against the first tape and bring the thread around

Stage 7.

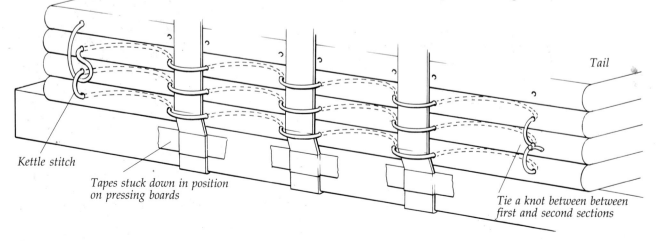

Head

Tail

Kettle stitch

Tapes stuck down in position on pressing boards

Tie a knot between between first and second sections

the tape, in through the third hole and out through the next. Continue in this way until the thread emerges from the head kettle stitch.

Take up any slack by pulling the thread parallel to the spine as shown at stage 6 on page 28.

Pass the needle through the head kettle stitch of the next section and repeat the procedure down the length of that section until the thread emerges from the tail kettle stitch. At this point the thread is knotted to the loose thread at the beginning.

To help reduce swelling gently tap the spine edges of each section with a hammer as the sewing progresses.

Stage 8

Continue sewing along the third section and, when the needle and thread emerge from the head kettle stitch, pull the thread tight and then loop it through the lower kettle stitch before sewing along the fourth section.

At the final kettle stitch, on the last section, the thread is knotted twice through the lower kettle stitch. Cut off the ends leaving about 10mm (^{3}/$_8$in) to spare.

Stage 8.

Stage 9.

Stage 9

When sewing a book in this manner, it is only possible to handle a relatively short length of thread at one time. From time to time it will be necessary to tie in a new thread using a small 'weaver's knot'.

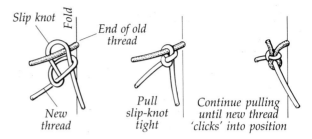

This knot is made by forming a slip-knot in the new thread, placing the loop over the end of the old thread at a point inside the book which will not pull through a hole. The knot is then pulled tight over the old thread until it clicks into position.

The bookblock will still have a certain amount of swelling in the spine. Knock up the bookblock at the top and spine edges and then gently hammer along the spine edge to reduce any swelling.

Note Swelling in the spine is inevitable due to folding and sewing. It should be reduced where possible at every stage, but as will be demonstrated, a slight swell in the spine helps the bookblock to be rounded.

Stage 10

Lay the bookblock flat on a board or the table, with the spine overlapping the edge, and set the spine and fore-edge square. Using PVA, glue-out the spine, rubbing the adhesive well in between the sections and tapes.

Place the bookblock between pressing blocks, and under a weight, while the glue sets for about half an hour.

Stage 10.

Stage 11.

Stage 11

When the glue has started to dry out the spine must be rounded. Draw the top and bottom sections forward (towards the fore-edge) and gently hammer along both sides of the spine. A slight swelling in the spine helps and, if your sewing is of the right tension, the spine will round in a gentle yet even curve.

Tip on the endpapers as shown on pages 34–35 and then leave the completed bookblock between pressing boards and under a heavy weight. When dry trim out the endpapers.

Lining-up

When the bookblock is thoroughly dry the spine must be lined-up with mull and kraft paper.

Lining-up with mull and kraft paper.

Apply a second, even coat of PVA to the spine.

Cut the piece of mull slightly shorter than the length of the spine but wide enough to overlap it by about 30mm (1¼in) on each side; place it across the spine.

Cut the kraft paper to the exact width and length of the spine, glue it out with paste and then stick it down on the spine. Rub it down with a damp sponge or rag. As the kraft paper dries it will shrink and adhere tightly to the spine.

Leave the book under a weight to dry. When it is completely dry trim out the mull by cropping the loose edges parallel with the spine and then cut the ends off at an angle.

Making the case

For this particular exercise the book is made in the quarter-bound style. However, any of the styles made in the previous chapter can be used but with a modification to allow for the extra width of the spine.

A strip of manila, or thin card, should be cut slightly wider than the width of the spine and the same length of the boards. The thickness of the boards and the size of the squares will depend on the size of the binding. For this project 2mm (about ³⁄₃₂in) thick boards are used.

The boards must be cut to allow at least 8–10mm (about ³⁄₈in) for the hinge at the spine. The squares should be 3–5mm (about ³⁄₁₆in).

Holding the boards and spine strip in position, wrap some waste paper around the spine and mark off positions for the edges of the spine strip and boards (see stage 2 on page 30). This measurement is vital when making the case.

To make the process easier, draw the exact positions of the spine strip and boards on the reverse of the cloth before gluing-out. Rub the case down well after gluing and pay particular attention to where the cloth folds into the spine.

Casing-in

Casing-in is achieved in the same manner as that described on pages 32–33, and the book is left to dry under a heavy weight.

Binding magazines

Sewing together magazines, periodicals or newspaper supplements requires a strong form of sewing structure. Magazines, in particular, are often constructed as a single section of many pages (the monthly-issue BBC *Wildlife* magazines used in this project are produced as a single fold of thirty-eight leaves – seventy-six printed pages – and are fastened with a single staple at the centre). A decision has to be made about how many issues will comfortably make one volume; for example, our magazine is too large and cumbersome to bind into year volumes. Books split into half-years, as in this project, may be a more practical solution. As a rough guide, the spine width of the bookblock should be limited to say 30–40mm (1¼–1¾in).

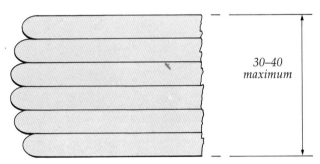

30–40 maximum

Limit the spine width of volumes to 30–40mm (1¼–1¾in).

Sewing through heavy paper and thick sections requires strong thread and wide tapes. The sewing method, therefore, differs slightly from that for the previous multi-section book. The endpapers are also made in a different way and are sewn into the bookblock as a section.

Preparation

Remove any staples or fasteners from the magazine sections.

Reduce any swelling in the folds of the magazine by hammering the folds as described at stage 1 on page 44. If time allows, the sections should be put under the heaviest weight you can find for a day or two. At the very least, rub the folds down well with a bone folder.

Materials

Six issues of magazines (or to a maximum thickness of 40mm (1¾in)). The BBC magazines are A4-size (about 8 x 12in).

Two folded sheets of coloured paper and two folded sheets of marbled paper for endpapers. (The folded sheets should be the same size as or slightly larger than the bookblock.)

Thick strong thread.

20mm (¾in) wide sewing tapes.

Mull.

Kraft paper.

Cover cloth for the spine and corners.

Cover paper.

One sheet of millboard or greyboard, 2mm (about ³/₃₂in) thick, sized to allow the cutting of two cover boards slightly larger than the bookblock, with the grain running head to tail.

Filling-in paper.

Two scrap pieces of board, slightly larger than the page size, for knocking up the sections.

Fresh paste and PVA.

Making the endpapers

There are many ways to make endpapers. 'Stiff-leaving' with a hand-made marbled paper is one traditional style. An alternative method is to use two folded sheets of coloured paper, tipped together, at each end of the bookblock. Both methods of making endpapers are described below.

Stiff-leaving marbled paper

Hand-made marbled paper is often marked on its underside during manufacture. Stiff-leaving will conceal these marks; the method involves gluing together two folded sheets of paper – one marbled, the other plain – to form a three-leaf section at each end of the bookblock. Particular care must be taken to ensure the grain direction of both sheets is head to tail.

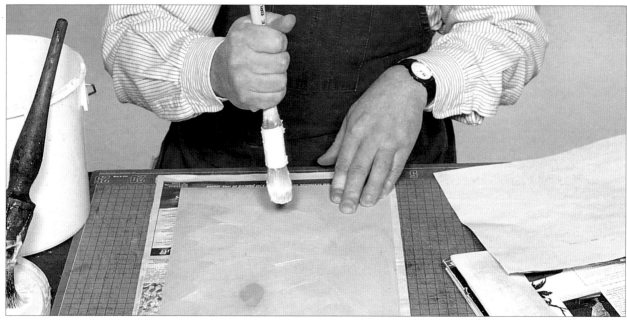

Stage 1.

Stage 2.

Adding strength to endpaper sections with mull.

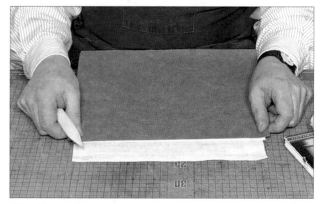

Attaching endpapers.

Stage 1

Using a piece of scrap newspaper between the fold, apply a thin layer of glue to one side of a folded sheet of the plain paper.

Stage 2

Glue-out a folded sheet of marbled paper (folded with the pattern on the inside) in a similar way and then carefully position it on to the glued surface of the plain paper, aligning the folded spine edges. To avoid cockling leave under a weight to dry.

Four-leaf coloured-paper endpapers

Apply a 5mm (¼in) strip of glue down the spine edge of one of the folded sheets in a similar manner to that described at stage 1 on page 34.

Place the second folded sheet on to the glued edge, carefully aligning all sides.

Adding strength to the endpaper sections

Although both types of endpapers are glued and sewn into the bookblock, added strength can be applied to these thin sections as follows.

Cut two strips of calico or linen about 50mm (2in) wide and slightly shorter than the length of the spine.

Apply a 5mm (¼in) strip of glue to one edge of the linen and stick to the last page of the first section (magazine). Use a bone folder to ensure a good smooth finish. Glue the second piece of linen in a similar way but in this instance glue it to the front page of the last section of the bookblock.

Attaching the endpapers

Apply a 5mm (¼in) strip of glue to the last page of the front endpaper section and attach it to the front of the first section, under the linen strengthening flap. Glue the front page of the back endpaper section in a similar way and attach to the back page of the last section of the bookblock, again under the linen strip.

Sewing the bookblock

The method of sewing bookblocks made up of magazines is essentially the same as that described on page 44–48. Magazines are usually very heavy and it is necessary to make a much stronger binding. Although the endpapers have been glued on to the first and last sections, when the bookblock is sewn they are treated as individual sections and sewn as such. Each endpaper section is sewn through the fold nearest the bookblock, taking care not to pierce the outer fold.

Mark up the bookblock as shown at stage 5 on page 46, and mount wide tapes on to a wooden block or the underside of the table.

Knock up the magazines, taking time to get them level. The different sections may vary in size and, if so, they should always be knocked up to the head.

Pierce holes with a bodkin as described at stage 6 on page 46. If the staple holes line up, then these can be incorporated into the sewing structure. However, it is more likely that new holes will have to be made.

Thread the needle and, starting at the tail kettle stitch, commence sewing the endpaper. Sew through the fold nearest the bookblock, taking the needle through the fold in the strip of linen as well. Work towards the kettle stitch at the head.

Pull the thread taut and begin to sew down the second section (the first magazine). When the needle emerges from the hole adjacent to the first tape, pass the thread through the loop in the section below as shown on the diagram. This will hold each section tightly together and help to reduce the swelling.

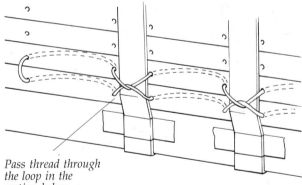

Pass thread through the loop in the section below

Forwarding

When the sewing is completed line-up the spine with mull and kraft paper as detailed on page 48, and case-in the bookblock to finish the project. In this exercise a comparatively plain cover in a half-bound style has been chosen to contrast with the highly patterned endpapers.

Large scrapbook or photograph album

Large 'Victorian-style' scrapbooks have many uses, from storing ephemera to displaying photographs. They are best made quite large and need to be of a strong construction.

The paper for the bookblock must be stiff and heavy enough to support the added contents, but not so stiff that the book cannot be opened flat. To compensate for the thickness of the material stuck on to the pages of the scrapbook, 'compensation guards' are incorporated into the structure of the bookblock. Two guards are fitted to each section of the bookblock. They are usually narrow strips of paper, the same weight as the actual pages; one is placed on the outside of the section, the other between the two folded leaves.

Materials

Large sheets of heavyweight paper.

Strong linen thread.

Sewing tapes.

Mull.

Kraft paper.

Covering materials: cloth and paper.

Boards, at least 2mm (about ³/₃₂in) in thickness.

Fresh glue.

Making the sections

Loose compensation guards

Fold two sheets of paper in half and use a bone folder to make a good crease. For this type of book a four-leaf section is normal.

Fold two 75mm (3in) strips of paper and using the bone folder make the crease. The width of the strips is not crucial, but if they are too small they can make sewing awkward.

Place one strip on the inside of the section and the other on the outside as illustrated below.

Alternative method using integral guards

Using paper that is about 40mm (1¹/₂in) wider than the single-page size, make a spine fold 40mm in from one edge. Make four such pages.

Interleave the folded pages to form the section, ensuring that there is a narrow strip between each full-size page as shown below.

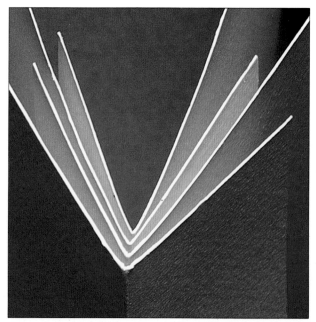

Loose compensation guards.

Integral compensation guards.

Making the bookblock

Make the required number of sections as detailed above.

Fold two full-size sheets in half and make a crease with the bone folder. These are for the endpapers and will not require compensation guards.

Temporarily secure the compensation guards to each section with paperclips.

Complete the sewing of the bookblock in a similar way to that for the magazines (see page 51).

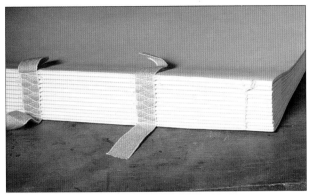

Sewn bookblock.

Making the case

The case for this type of book needs to be quite substantial. A 2mm ($^{1}/_{16}$in) thick millboard is used for this project. Again the cover style is open to choice but remember to keep the proportions right – the larger the cover sides the wider the spine cloth.

Casing-in

Casing-in a large wedge-shaped scrapbook needs to be carried out in a special way. The size and weight of the book can make handling difficult, and provision must be made to support the bookblock when it hangs over the edge of your table.

Stage 1

Glue-out the endpaper and pull the cover board over in the normal way, ensuring that the squares are equal at head and tail.

Turn the book over and, opening the bookblock slightly, adjust the position of the endpaper and rub down well.

Place the completed cover board flat on the edge of the table, with the inside facing down and the bookblock hanging over the edge. Support the weight of the bookblock in some way – a table with a drawer unit is ideal.

Define the hinge between the spine and cover with a bone folder. Place a length of thick hemp or some 5mm ($^{1}/_{4}$in) dowel along the hinge, between the cover and the spine, and then place a board and heavy weight on top as illustrated.

Stage 1.

Leave the weight on for a few hours to let the glue dry and then repeat the procedure for the other endpaper and cover board.

Stage 2

Close the covers and tie a heavy cord round the book, with the cord in the spine groove. Place a large pressing board over the top of the book, put it under a heavy weight and leave for twenty-four hours.

Stage 2.

RIGHT: *Photographic album, made as a multi-section binding, showing compensation guards between each leaf.*

SINGLE-LEAF BINDINGS

Not all books are made from folded sheets of paper or sections. Sometimes the paper is in single sheets and a different method of binding must be used. This chapter shows how single leaves, such as a typed report or thesis, can be sewn into strong bookblocks. It also demonstrates how the most common single-leaf book, the paperback, can be repaired and, if necessary, rebound. The final exercise shows a completely different approach: a Japanese binding using limp covers and very little adhesive.

A typed report

The introduction of mass-produced books, and the paperback in particular, meant that publishers could no longer afford to have books sewn in the traditional manner. The pages are simply glued together at the spine edge and then cased-in to thin card covers. This method of making books is known in the trade as 'perfect' binding.

This inappropriately named style of binding actually had its origins back in the nineteenth century. Many of the early lithographic colour-plate books were bound as single leaves, using 'caoutchouc' (or India rubber) as the adhesive on the spine. These early books have rarely survived intact, and although modern glues have been developed for the purpose, even new books bound in this way still tend to fall apart after a few years.

To make a stronger binding for this type of book a particular form of sewing can be used. Books made in this way will never open as flat as the sewn sections of folded sheets but, provided that the paper is not too thick, it is quite possible to make good strong bindings.

Making the bookblock

Stage 1

Collate the typed pages, checking to ensure that everything is in the right position. Place the paper together between two boards and knock the edges up to the head and spine as shown on page 45.

Keeping the block of paper as square as possible, lay it on its side, face up, and put a heavy weight on top.

Mark up the spine for sewing. The position of the kettle stitches should be about 15mm (⁵⁄₈in) from the top of the book and a little more, say 20mm (³⁄₄in), from the tail. Draw three lines equi-spaced between the kettle stitches.

Move the bookblock, with the weight still on top, so that it slightly overhangs the edge of the table. Alternatively, if you have a vice, clamp the bookblock together with the two boards in the jaws of the vice with the spine uppermost.

Using a fine-toothed saw, make three saw slots, about 1–2mm (¹⁄₁₆in) deep, along the lines drawn between the kettle stitches. These will hold the

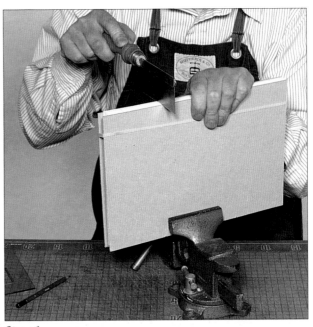

Stage 1.

cords and help to keep the bookblock square when the book is being sewn.

Stage 2

Remove the weight (or remove the bookblock from the vice) and divide the report into sections of equal numbers of pages (say sixteen leaves per section).

Knock up each section at the head and use a strong paperclip to hold them in place.

Stage 2.

Stage 3.

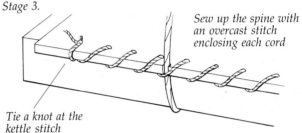

Sew up the spine with an overcast stitch enclosing each cord

Tie a knot at the kettle stitch

Using a bodkin punch a series of holes 10mm (³/₈in) apart and 4–5mm (³/₁₆in) in from the spine edge. Avoid placing holes close to the sawn slots.

Stage 3

Secure the cords to the underside of a wooden pressing board or table in a similar way to that described for tapes (see page 46), spacing them to match the sawn slots.

Lay the last section of the report on the block, aligning the sawn slots with the cords.

Using a needle and thin thread, take the needle through the tail kettle stitch and tie a knot.

Sew up the length of the spine using an overcast stitch, enclosing each cord as it is reached, and tie a knot around the head kettle stitch.

Stage 4

Gently tap the spine edge with a hammer to flatten the sewing thread and reduce any swelling.

Lay the second section on top and repeat the procedure, working down to the tail, knotting the sections together at the head and tail stitches.

The sewn-in cords and the knots at head and tail provide 'anchors' that keep the book level.

The bookblock can now be forwarded in the normal way.

Stage 4.

Paperbacks

Almost everyone has a collection of paperbacks. They are often treasured possessions that become well thumbed and dilapidated through frequent use. The inevitable result is often loose pages and detached covers.

The sewn-in method used for the typed report is inappropriate for this type of book. Overcasting changes the whole character of the original book; it makes it more bulky and the original cover may not fit properly. In any case, most paperbacks do not have enough margin in the spine for overcasting and, if the paper is old and brittle, the paper would tend to break up during sewing.

The method described in this section retains the original character of the book and allows the covers, if still existing, to be used again. Where the original covers, or part of them, have been lost a case can be made.

REPAIRING A WRAPPER

If the wrapper is torn or weak at the spine it can be restored quite easily. The wrapper of the book used for this project, *Histoire de France*, had a detached and torn front cover, and a very badly damaged spine. In some cases the wrapper may be beyond simple repair and a new case will be needed (see page 64).

> **Materials**
>
> *The damaged paperback.*
>
> *A strip of calico (to repair the spine).*
>
> *Fresh paste and PVA.*

Stage 1

Carefully remove the remnants of the wrapper from the bookblock using the flat blade of a penknife. When working on the spine you might find it easier to hold the book in the jaws of a small vice. If the pieces of cover are badly creased flatten out the creases with a bone folder. Placing them under a weight will help.

Stage 2

Cut the calico slightly oversize on the length and 25mm (1in) wider than the spine. Glue-out the strip of calico with paste and lay down the pieces of the spine, making the fit as good as possible. Again, use the bone folder to iron out any creases.

Stage 3

Place the front and back covers in position, adding more paste as necessary, and rub down with the bone folder. Leave the repaired wrapper under a weight to dry and then, using a straight-edge, trim off the excess calico.

Lay the wrapper with the inside uppermost on the table. Position the bookblock flush with the front cover and mark with a pencil the position of the spine edge. This is important, as the original crease may have become 'lost' in the course of repair.

Using a straight-edge positioned against the pencil marks, make a crease with the point of a bone folder.

Stage 4

Lay the bookblock, face up, on a pressing board or table so that the spine edge overhangs slightly. Position the wrapper square to the fore-edge and hold in place with a pressing board and heavy weight. Using the bone folder, coax the wrapper down over the edge of the spine.

Stage 5

Lift the cover and glue-out the spine with a liberal application of PVA. Burnish the spine with a bone folder to achieve a good adhesion. Leave to dry.

Stage 6

When the spine is dry, remove the weight and pressing board. Turn the book over and gently pull the back cover over, creasing with the bone folder at the spine edge.

Stage 1.

Stage 2.

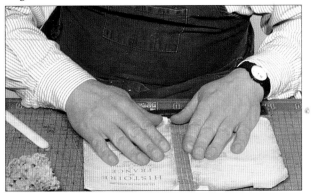

Stage 3.

Stage 4.

Stage 5.

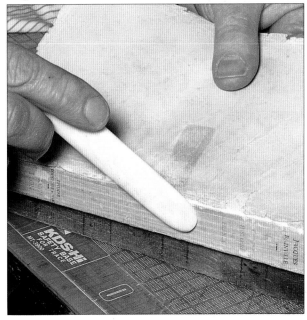

Stage 6.

REBINDING A PAPERBACK

If the bookblock is starting to come apart, with some loose pages, it is better to 'pull' the whole binding. Do not be tempted to tip-in the odd page – others will eventually come out and you will not have remedied the situation. For this exercise a much loved but rather battered copy of Orwell's *Nineteen Eighty-Four* is rebound.

> **Materials**
>
> *Paperback book or similar perfect-bound book in need of restoration.*
>
> *Thin hemp cord or thick sewing thread.*
>
> *Mull.*
>
> *Calico, or thin paper.*
>
> *PVA.*
>
> *Silicone-release or greaseproof paper.*
>
> *Four pieces of waste board.*
>
> *Covering materials, paper or cloth.*
>
> *Thin boards for the covers.*
>
> *Manila, or similar thick paper.*
>
> *Endpapers.*

Stage 1.

Stage 2.

Preparing the bookblock

Stage 1

If the cover is still attached it must be removed. A penknife, not too sharp, is the best tool for this task. Pull back the outer cover and ease the blade between the wrapper and the spine. With patience and gentle coaxing, the wrapper can be parted from the spine intact. It is easier to work on the spine with the book held in the vice.

Stage 2

Remove as much of the old glue from the spine by scraping gently with the blade of the penknife. Scrape away what you can, and then take the book apart, page by page. Open the pages, one at a time, and pull each sheet horizontally away from the spine.

Using the thumb and forefinger, strip any remaining glue from the spine edge of each page. This may sound a long procedure, but in reality it will only take about ten minutes.

Use a bone folder to flatten out any pages that are creased.

Tip on a waste sheet to the first and last page. A few small spots of paste or PVA on the spine edge of each sheet is all that is needed to secure these waste sheets. Their purpose is to protect the bookblock from glue and they will be removed later. Trim the waste sheet to the size of the page.

Stage 3

Knock up all the pages and make the bookblock as square as possible.

Take the two larger waste boards, knock these up to the fore-edge and then place the book, with spine uppermost, between the jaws of a vice and tighten. Check again that the pages are level at the fore-edge, head and tail. If you are not satisfied, take the bookblock out of the vice and knock up the pages

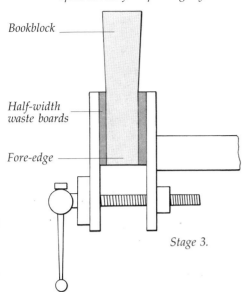

Spine should fan open slightly

Bookblock

Half-width
waste boards

Fore-edge

Stage 3.

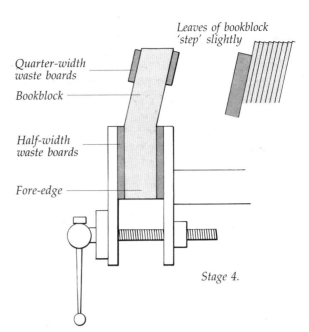

*Leaves of bookblock
'step' slightly*

Quarter-width
waste boards

Bookblock

Half-width
waste boards

Fore-edge

Stage 4.

again. The spine should fan open slightly when held in the vice.

Stage 4

The PVA glue should be thick and not runny. If using it straight from the tub, brush some out on the lid of the glue pot, or on a piece of waste paper, until it becomes 'good and sticky'.

Grip the spine with the two smaller pieces of waste board and bend the bookblock slightly to one side. This will cause the paper to 'step' very slightly as shown in the diagram.

Stage 5

Hold the bookblock firmly in this position and glue all along the spine. If the glue is very sticky, it is best to stipple the glue rather than brush it. Ensure that the whole surface is covered.

Push the bookblock the other way so that the paper steps in the opposite direction. Repeat the gluing operation, then release the boards and allow the bookblock to return to the vertical position.

Stage 6

Grip the two waste boards to squeeze the bookblock again and remove most of the surplus glue with the forefinger. At the same time rub the remaining thin layer of glue evenly over the spine. If the glue is still runny, there is a danger that too much pressure will cause the glue to penetrate the

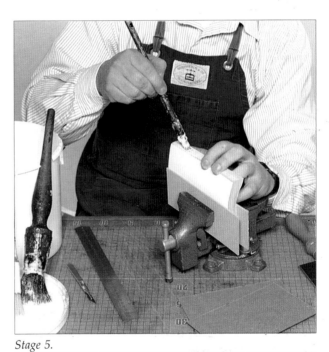

Stage 5.

Stage 6.

bookblock. Let the bookblock dry for a minute or two before removing from the vice.

Remove the waste boards and place the bookblock between pressing boards lined with greaseproof paper. Apply a heavy weight and allow to dry thoroughly.

Each page of the book is now held at the spine edge with a thin strip of glue. There should be just sufficient to hold the paper in place: excessive glue could penetrate too far and prevent the book from opening properly.

Stage 7

Add strength to the bookblock by recessing threads or thin hemp into slots sawn into the spine. Place the book back in the vice between boards, and saw two or three shallow slots across the spine, as shown on page 58, but at an angle of about 45°. The depth of the slots should be just sufficient to drop in a thread flush with the spine.

Press the thread well in to the slots, keeping it as tight as possible.

Trim away the excess thread and line-up the spine with a thick layer of PVA, mull and kraft paper as described on page 48.

If the bookblock is being recased into the original wrapper, the mull should be cut flush with the edges of the spine, and the wrapper fitted as shown on pages 60–61.

Rebinding old bookblocks in this way inevitably results in a spine that is wider than the original and

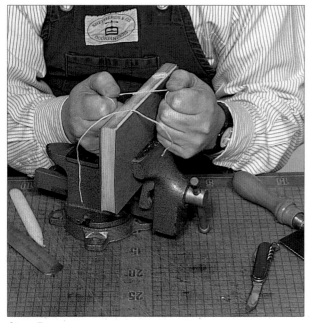

Stage 7.

it will be difficult to fit it into the original wrapper. To some extent this can be guarded against by pressing the bookblock under a heavy weight, but some swelling is bound to occur. If you do want to use the old wrapper, ensure that any 'shortfall' in the recreased wrapper is concealed at the back of the book.

Making a case

The basic case can be made in the normal way and, if substantial parts of the wrapper survive, they can be incorporated into the binding.

This is best achieved by 'recessing' the old covers into the new boards. Recessing will prevent the paper 'catching' and will greatly improve the visual appearance of the book. Only the front cover of the original wrapper of *Nineteen Eighty-Four* existed and this is recessed into the new cover. The covering materials should blend with the colour scheme of the old wrapper. If you use paper as the covering material it will need a reinforcing strip on the inside of the spine.

Stage 1

Use thin card for the cover boards and cut with narrow squares (see diagram on page 30).

Cut a back strip from the similar card, the same height as the cover and slightly wider than the thickness of the bookblock.

Line the inside of each board with a sheet of thin bank paper.

Position the piece(s) of the old wrapper on the board(s). No part of the old wrapper should overlap the outer edges of the boards or back strip. Draw a pencil line around each piece; mark the reverse side of the front board with an F.

Stage 2

Using paper that is the same thickness as the old wrapper, cut out rectangles that are slightly larger than the covers.

Position the pieces of the old wrapper on these and once again draw a pencil line around the shapes. The grain direction of the paper must run from head to tail.

Cut out the drawn shapes using a sharp blade, following the outside edges of the pencil lines. The resulting recess should be slightly larger than the pieces of wrapper.

Stage 1.

Stage 2.

Check the cut-out shapes against the pieces of the old wrapper and make any necessary alterations. The shapes should now marry with the pencil lines on the new boards.

Turn over the cut-outs, carefully glue them out and then position them on the boards, aligning the pencil marks with the cut-outs. Burnish down with a bone folder, remove any excess glue and then place under a weighted pressing board to dry. When dry, trim off the surplus all round.

Stage 3

The boards are now ready to be covered. Make the case, using the full-binding style described on pages 38–41, but before weighting it down to dry continue with the following steps.

With a bone folder, or similar pointed instrument, find the shape of the cut-outs beneath the cover material and gently press the covering material into the shapes.

Glue-out the pieces of the old wrapper and fit them into their correct positions. They should lie flush with the covering material.

Rub down through greaseproof paper, pressing hard on the pieces of the old covers. Leave under a very heavy weight to dry.

Remove the waste sheets from the bookblock, attach endpapers and case-in to complete the project.

Stage 3.

Japanese binding

This very decorative style is based on a method commonly used in Japan and provides a simple solution to the problem of binding single leaves. It involves a technique called 'stab sewing' which uses the thread or ribbon as a decorative feature of the outside cover. For reasons that will become obvious the paper for the bookblock should not be too heavy or stiff.

The technique can be applied in a variety of ways and books can be made from a wide range of materials. Japanese decorative papers make ideal covering materials, but literally anything from wrapping paper to furnishing fabrics can be used. Very little glue is needed for this binding as it is the form of sewing that holds the book together. In the beginning, however, some glue should be used as directed.

Materials

Single sheets of paper for the bookblock.

Decorative paper for the covers and endpapers.

Two sheets of plain paper, slightly larger than the bookblock leaves.

Coloured thread or ribbon.

Making the bookblock

Knock up the pages of the bookblock, and designate one of the long edges as the spine.

Place the bookblock flat on the table, with the spine just overlapping the edge, and secure in place with a pressing board and weight. The spine edge should fan apart very slightly.

Apply a thin layer of PVA to the spine edge, leave for a few minutes to become tacky and then move the bookblock to one side, still under a weight, to dry completely.

Tip-in two sheets of contrasting endpapers at each end of the bookblock. Leave under a weight to dry and then trim the endpapers to size.

Making the wrapper

The wrapper is completely different from any of the other projects and is made as three separate components: two side pieces and a spine.

Stage 1

Cut the two sheets of plain paper 2mm ($^1/_{16}$in) wider than the bookblock and 4mm ($^1/_8$in) longer.

Cut two pieces of the decorative paper 30mm ($1^1/_4$in) larger than the bookblock in both directions.

Lay one sheet of decorative paper face down on to a piece of scrap newspaper and then place one of the plain sheets centrally on top.

Cut off the corners of the decorative paper to within 2mm ($^1/_{16}$in) of the plain paper.

Glue-out the exposed edges of the decorative paper, turn in each edge, pinching the corners to make a neat join, and then use a bone folder to complete the seal.

Stage 2

Cut another piece of decorative paper (a contrasting one if you wish) large enough to overlap the spine of the bookblock at the sides and at the head and tail. The overlap can vary with the size of the book, but should be no more than 5mm ($^3/_{16}$in).

Place the bookblock in the jaws of a small vice with the spine edge upwards.

Glue-out the spine cover paper and place it in a central position on the spine of the bookblock. Fold down the side edges, rubbing down with a bone folder. At the head and tail turn down the ends to form a cap. Apply a little more glue to the two 'wings' and fold them in.

Apply a 5mm ($^1/_4$in) strip of glue to the spine edge of the inside of each side piece (as for tipping-in) and attach the side pieces to the bookblock. These need to be flush with the spine and overlap the other three sides to form even squares.

Stage 1.

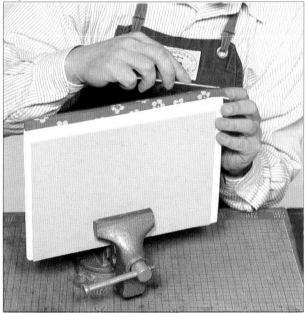

Stage 2.

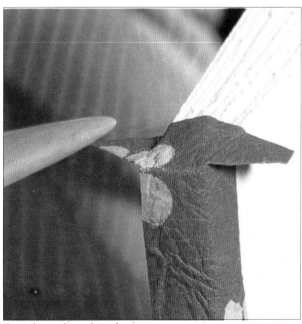

Turn down the ends to form a cap.

Stage 1.

Stage 2.

Sewing the book

This decorative form of sewing is completely different from any described earlier and the route taken by the thread is shown in the diagram below.

Stage 1

Using a bodkin and hammer, pierce four holes through the complete book, 10mm (³/₈in) in from the spine. The position of these holes can vary enormously, but in this binding they are positioned at equal spaces down the length of the spine.

Stage 2

Thread and knot the needle using a contrasting coloured thread or narrow ribbon. Starting at the tail of the book, pass the needle through the first hole from the underside, around the spine, then through the same hole again to form a loop. Take the needle down through the next hole, around the spine again and back through the second hole. Repeat for the third and fourth holes.

Take the thread over the top of the book, down through the fourth hole and up through the next. Now take the thread down through the second hole, up through the first, and around the tail of the book to the beginning. Complete the sewing by tying a knot over the first hole and, using the blunt end of a needle, conceal the knot inside the hole.

Apply a 10mm (³/₈in) strip of glue to the fore-edge of the end papers and attach them to the inside of the side wrappers, rubbing them down well with your fingers. Leave the book under a weight to dry.

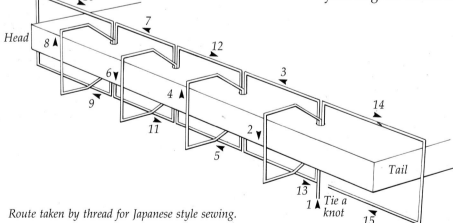

Route taken by thread for Japanese style sewing.

RIGHT: *Paperbacks, bound typed reports and books made in the Japanese style are all single-leaf bindings.*

PORTFOLIOS

A portfolio is a practical way of storing paper, particularly in situations where a sewn binding is inappropriate. A collection of prints or drawings, for example, needs to be retained as individual sheets; putting them in a portfolio is a good method of keeping them together.

Portfolios

A portfolio is made much like the case of a book, but it has flaps attached to the inside lower board to enclose and protect the contents. In this project the flaps are made as a envelope, entirely separately from the outside case, which is then attached to the inside of the back cover.

Portfolios can be made to any size and often need to be quite large. Large ones require a heavy covering material such as a buckram bookcloth.

Particular care should be taken with the inside linings, and it is well worth taking the time to fill-in and ensure flat surfaces.

If the portfolio is being made for a specific collection of items, the sizes of the individual pieces are calculated by working from the inside outwards (the sheet size and thickness of the contents). This means that the inside envelope must be constructed first.

Making the inside envelope

The inside envelope comprises four pieces: the back, two side flaps and a fore-edge flap. The grain direction of each piece must be the same. The shapes of these pieces, and their positions relative to each other, are shown in the diagram.

Before cutting out any materials, measure the length and breadth of the largest sheet to be enclosed and the thickness of the total number of sheets.

Cut a piece of the thin card or manila a few millimetres (about $^1/_4$in) larger than the size of the contents. This card is the back of the envelope and the corners must be perfectly square.

Cut three other pieces of card for the flaps. The length of the side flaps should be the same as the short edge of the back, and that of the fore-edge flap the same as the long edge. Grain direction must be the same throughout. The width of the side flaps

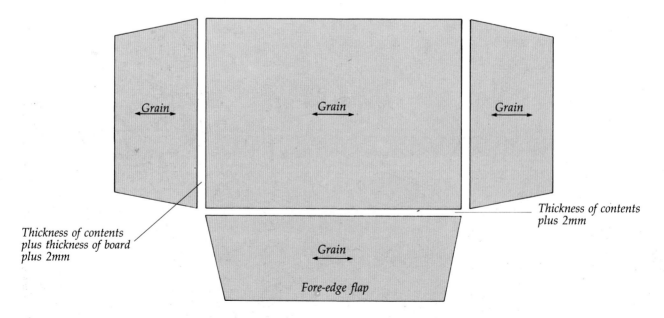

Thickness of contents plus thickness of board plus 2mm

Grain

Grain

Grain

Grain

Fore-edge flap

Thickness of contents plus 2mm

Shapes and relative sizes of boards for the inside envelope.

should be such that, when folded in, they do not overlap. The fore-edge flap can be as wide as you like but is generally limited to half the width of the back piece. The ends of each flap should be tapered.

Add about 2mm (1/16in) to the thickness of the contents. This will be the width of the joint on the fore-edge flap.

Add the thickness of the board to the measurement determined above. This will be the width of the joints between the back and the side flaps.

Having determined these measurements, cut three pieces of cloth for the joints. They should be slightly longer than their respective flaps and wide enough to overlap the boards by at least 20mm (3/4in) on each side. As always, the cloth must be cut with the grain in the same direction as the boards.

Glue-out each piece of cloth in turn and place the card flaps in position. Leave to dry.

When the joints are dry trim the excess cloth flush to the edge of the flaps and, where they overlap on the fore-edge, mitre the cloth at 45° to the corners. Remove surplus layers of cloth.

Cut pieces of the covering paper slightly oversize but with one long edge perfectly straight.

Glue-out each piece and pitch the long straight edge on to the flaps (see page 31) so that it just overlaps the spine cloth. When dry, the paper is cut flush to the card.

Making the case

Stage 1

Cut the cover boards from the thick board, ensuring that they are square and are at least 5mm (1/4in) larger than the envelope in both directions.

Cut a piece of manila, or thick paper, the same length as the boards and slightly wider than the full thickness of the envelope. This will line the inside of the spine.

Cut a piece of cloth for the spine. It must be 30mm (1 1/4in) longer than the spine and wide enough to allow an overlap of 30mm (1 1/4in) on each cover board, plus the full thickness of the envelope, plus the thickness of two cover boards.

Glue-out the spine cloth and lay down the cover boards in the appropriate positions. Turn-in the ends and rub well down with a bone folder.

Cut out the cover paper and pitch on to the boards as described on page 31.

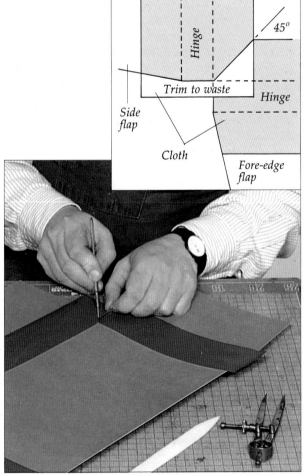

Mitre the cloth at 45° to the corners.

Stage 1.

Stage 2.

Stage 2

Using a chisel or sharp knife, cut a slit in the middle of each of the cover boards, about 15mm (⅝in) in from the fore-edge. The width of the slits should be the same as the width of the tapes.

Stage 3

Thread a 400mm (16in) length of tape through each slot and secure about 20mm (¾in) of it on the inside with a spot of PVA. Close the slot over the tape by tapping with a hammer.

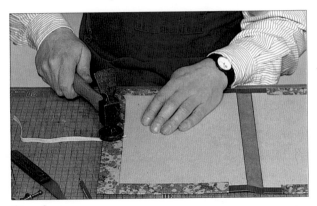

Stage 3.

74

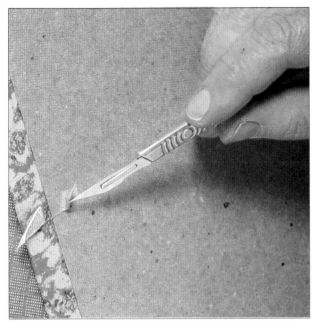

Stage 4.

Stage 5.

Stage 4

Draw a pencil line around the end of the tape and then, using a sharp blade, cut into the cover board around the pencilled shape. Carefully lift out the tape together with a layer of board roughly the same thickness as the tape. Remove the piece of board from the tape.

Stage 5

Apply a little glue to the recess, replace the tape and rub down with a bone folder.

Make two similar slots in the side flaps of the inside envelope in a similar manner to that described in stages 2–5.

Recessing the tapes is not absolutely necessary, but it does make for a smoother finish.

Filling-in

Before gluing the envelope into position, you should fill-in the inside of the cover boards with sugar paper and then cover them with a contrasting paper. The same paper can also be used to cover the inside surfaces of the envelope.

Filling-in before lining with a cover paper is always well worth the effort, as the appearance of the inside boards is greatly improved by a flat surface. This is particularly true in the case of portfolios, where the surfaces tend to be quite large and the covering materials are thick.

Stage 1.

Stage 1

Cut two pieces of sugar paper and fill-in the insides of the case (see pages 38–40). Leave under a weight to dry.

Glue-out the whole underside surface of the envelope and position it on the inside of one of the cover boards, with the fore-edge flap to the front. Rub down well and place under heavy weights until it is thoroughly dry.

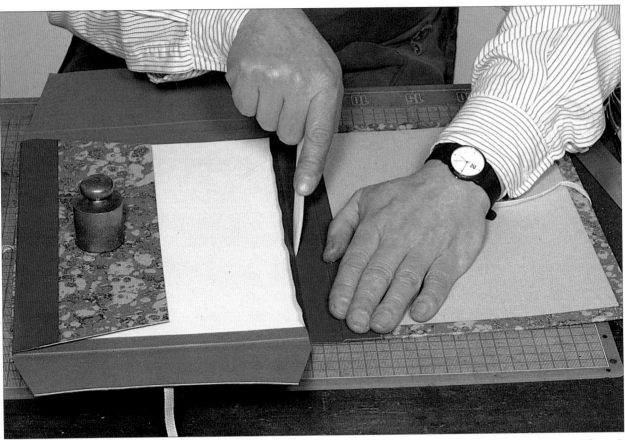

Stage 2

Cut a piece of cloth to line the inside of the spine of the outer case. It should be slightly shorter than the length of the spine and wide enough to overlap generously on both sides.

Glue-out the cloth, position along the inside of the spine and, using a bone folder, rub it down well, especially into the spine creases. Where the cloth overlaps the paper on the inside of the envelope, the materials should be cut at 45° and excess layers removed.

Cover the inside of the flaps of the envelope with pieces of contrasting paper, taking each piece across the flap spine on to the back piece. Rub each piece down well into the creases. Mitre the corners where the individual pieces overlap and remove excess material.

Fill-in the back piece of the envelope as detailed above.

Cut two rectangular pieces of paper to cover the inside panels, glue-out and paste them down, rubbing them with a soft cloth or through a clean sheet of waste paper.

Lay the portfolio open on a flat surface and cover with weights. Leave for twenty-four hours.

Tie the tapes in a bow and judge by eye an adequate length. To prevent fraying, cut a V-shape in the end of each tape.

An alternative style

A variation on the above method incorporates the fore-edge flap into the outside case. This limits the design of the outer cover but makes the overall construction of the portfolio stronger.

The inside envelope is made with only side flaps. The measurement of the two joints must allow for the thickness of the fore-edge flap.

Once the inside envelope has been constructed, the outside cover is made up as before, but with no extra margin at the fore-edge square. The fore-edge flap is attached to the outside case with cloth.

The envelope is pitched into position with glue, and held securely in place by cloth linings at both the spine and the fore-edge joint.

RIGHT: *Use bold patterns on your portfolios. The blue striped one shown is made to the alternative style described above.*

Glossary

Every craft has its own special language; a glossary of words and phrases that, from an outsider's point of view, can be confusing. Bookbinding certainly has its own share of specialist terms and, although they have been kept to a minimum in this book, the use of some of them is necessary.

Head

Fore-edge

Spine

Tail

Squares

Endpaper

Case

Bookblock

Bookblock – a trade term for the paper contents of the book, as distinct from the outside cover.

Case – the outside cover of the book, usually constructed from two boards and covered in cloth and paper.

Casing-in – the process of attaching the book-block to the case.

Endpapers – the first and last leaves of the bookblock, often made from coloured or patterned paper.

Finishing – titling and decorating book covers.

Fore-edge – the front edge of the book, so called because in early times books were placed on shelves with the spine innermost.

Forwarding – a trade term for the processes of binding a book up to the finishing stage.

Full binding – a binding where the entire case is covered with a single material, normally a cloth.

Grain direction – nearly all materials are made from fibres which lie in predominantly one direction.

Greyboard (pulpboard) – available from bookbinding suppliers and art and craft shops. Greyboard is manufactured chiefly from waste fibre and is less dense than millboard. It is available in a range of thicknesses, all of which can be cut quite easily with a knife. Its strength and durability can be greatly improved by lining each side with a good-quality paper before use.

Guards – strips of paper that are incorporated into the bookblock to create extra swell at the spine. They are used to compensate for the later addition of photographs, as in an album.

Half binding – a binding where the spine and corners (or the complete fore-edge) are covered with one material and the rest of the boards with another.

Hardboard and thin plywood – available from DIY shops and builders' merchants. These boards are too thick for most bookbinding purposes, but can be useful for making large portfolios. Hardboard tends to crack easily and should be lined with a good-quality heavy paper prior to use.

Head – the top edge of the book (when stood upright).

Leaf – a single sheet of paper in a book (two pages). A sheet folded in half will have two leaves and hence four pages.

Millboard – only available from bookbinding suppliers. This is the best-quality bookbinding board and is available in a range of thicknesses. It is a dense fibre-board and the thicker sheets are quite difficult to cut without special board-cutting equipment. However, boards up to 2mm (¹⁄₁₆in) in thickness can be cut with a sharp craft knife and straight-edge.

Page – one side of a leaf.

Paste – an adhesive made from flour and water.

Perfect binding – a method of binding single leaves together using only glue.

Pitching – the action of glueing paper to cover boards.

PVA (polyvinyl acetate) – sometimes known in the trade as 'white glue', a flexible quick-drying adhesive.

Quarter binding – a binding where the spine area of the book is covered with one material and the rest of the case with another.

Sections (or signatures) – a set of folded sheets of paper as prepared for sewing.

Silicone-release paper – a paper treated with silicone to which adhesive will not adhere.

Single-section binding – a book made from only one set of folded pages; limited to very small books.

Spine – the back edge of the book (the part visible when a book is placed on a shelf).

Squares – the amount that the case boards overlap the bookblock at the head, tail and fore-edge, thus protecting the edges of the paper.

Tail – The bottom edge of a book.

Tipping-in/on – a commonly used term to describe the attachment of paper or other materials to another surface by means of a narrow strip of adhesive (usually about 5mm (¹⁄₄in) wide).

Weaver's knot – a non-slip knot used for joining two pieces of sewing thread.

Full binding

Half binding

Quarter binding

Index